word
power

Anne Rooney
Illustrated by Debi Ani

Big Fish

For my daughter, Lauren

First published in the UK in 2001 by
Big Fish, an imprint of C&B Children's Books,
London House, Great Eastern Wharf,
Parkgate Road, London SW11 4NQ
www.bigfishonline.co.uk

ISBN 1 903174 59 7

British Library Cataloguing in Publication Data
for this book is available from the British Library

Printed in China

Project Manager: Honor Head
Project Editor: Paul Dowswell
Designer: Angela Ashton
Illustrator: Debi Ani

CONTENTS

Starting off 4

Back to basics 11

Story go-round 17

Top secret 25

Let's party 30

Nice notes 37

Drama queens (and kings) 41

All I want is... 46

Thank you very much for... 53

Wanted – good posters 57

STARTING OFF

If you've got a PC or a Mac with Word on it, you can use this book to make lots of cool documents. Each chapter starts with a list telling you what's in it, like this:

LEARN TO...

- use this book
- add pictures to text
- find out what's on screen
- start up Word
- use your printer

What's inside

If you're sick of writing out thank-you letters, get your computer to help you. And if you're bored with dreary, black titles on your work, add sparkling text that glitters on the screen. Planning a party? Print whizzy invitations, placemarkers and labels for party bags. If your little brother or sister is always snooping around your secret diary or messages to your friends, you can learn how to write in a secret code.

Adding images

To do some of these things you will need pictures on the computer. You can make these yourself with a painting program (if you have one), or you can use clip art – ready-made pictures you get on a CD-ROM or from the World Wide Web. There is some clip art included with Word. If you've got a scanner or a digital camera, you can use them to get pictures too.

Printing it out

If you do a bright, colourful document, you'll probably want to print it out in colour. But if you don't have a colour printer, make sure all your pictures are outlines that you can colour in yourself after you've printed your work. If you use colour pictures but print them in black and white they will come out in mushy shades of grey – yuk!

WHIZZ KIDS

All you need is here in the book – but there are extra bits and pieces you can get from the Whizz Kids website, and links there you can follow to find other useful stuff. Go to www.bigfishonline.co.uk/whizzkids

5

Let's get going

When you turn on the computer, you will need to wait a moment for it to get ready. It has to wake up and get itself sorted before it can begin work.
Don't press any buttons or keys on the keyboard while it is doing this, just wait until the screen display stops changing.

Start up Word

The computer doesn't know what you want to do until you tell it by starting a program. You can start up a program in one of three ways:

- If you have an 'Office' toolbar, click the Word button on it.

- If someone has set up a short-cut icon on the desktop, double-click on it (click the left-hand mouse button twice, quickly).

- Choose it from the 'Programs' menu. To do this you'll need to use the 'Start' menu.

The first two are easiest, but if you can't find a toolbar or shortcut, you'll need to use the 'Start' menu.

To do this, move the pointer over the 'Start' button in the bottom left-hand corner of the screen and click the left-hand mouse button once to display the menu.

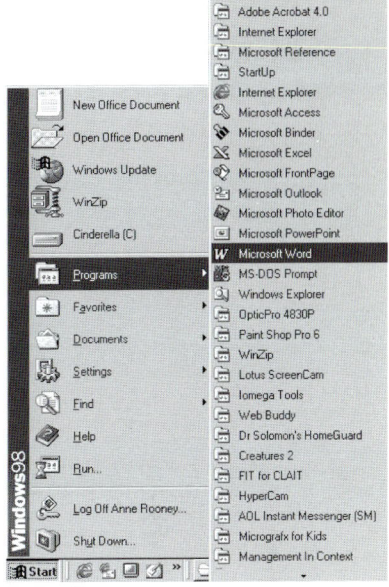

What's on the menu?

A menu is a list of options you can choose. Pick the one you want by clicking on it. Now move the pointer over the line 'Programs'. When you do this, the line changes colour and another menu appears to the right – the 'Programs' menu. It may be quite long. In this you should be able to find and click on 'Microsoft Word'. After a few seconds, Word will start up and you'll be ready to go. There will be a blank page for you to start work with – so let's get going!

Take a look around

Word will start a new document for you as soon as it is loaded. Then you can do what you want with it.

If you've used Word before, you can skip this section. If not, read on!

What's on the screen

The new document doesn't have any words in it, but has some other bits and pieces you should have a quick look at. If you look at the screen you'll see something like the picture below. Don't worry if it doesn't look exactly the same, as some grown-up might have changed the settings. But it will have a line of words across the top. These are the names of the menus.

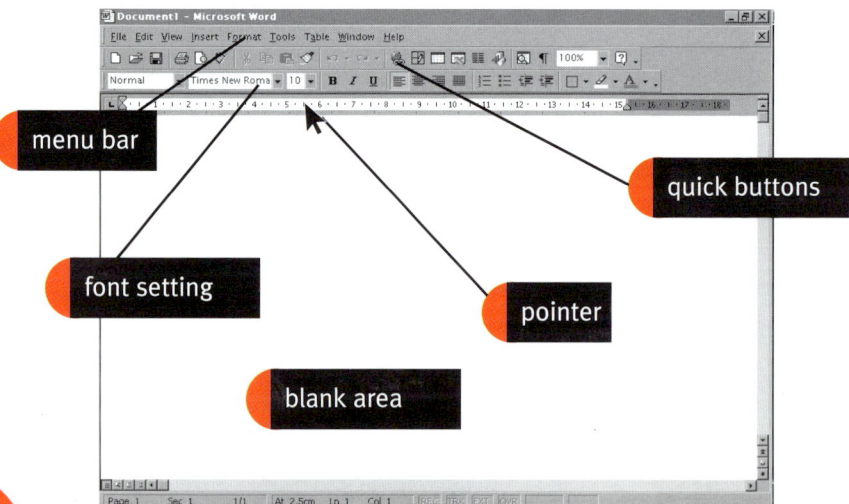

Working with menus

If you move the pointer over a menu name and click the left-hand mouse button, the menu pops down for you to choose something. Click on the option you want to pick, or click anywhere outside the menu to make it go away.

Quick buttons

Below the menu line will be one or more rows of buttons. These are quicker ways to get to some of the choices in the menus. Below this is another line that shows some settings, too, such as the font (design of letters) you are using. Don't worry about any of these for now. You'll find out how to use some of them as you need them.

Fill in the blank

Underneath all this is a big blank area for you to type what you want. This is the bit you are going to use first. There is a little flashing line in the blank area. It's called the cursor or caret. It shows you where the text you type will appear. Since there isn't anything in your document, it will appear at the beginning.

The pictures in this book show what you will see if you have Word 2000. If you have a different version of Word, you will still be able to do most of the things, but the screens will look a bit different sometimes. Word 2000 tries to keep the menus tidy by hiding things it doesn't think you will need. If you can't see the option you need in the menu, move the pointer onto the downward pointing double arrow ⁀ at the bottom and wait a moment, or click, and more options will appear.

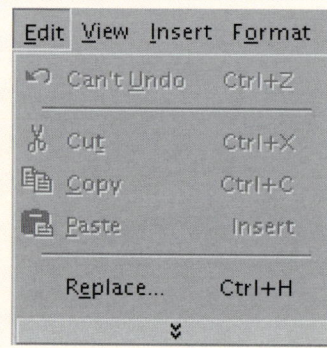

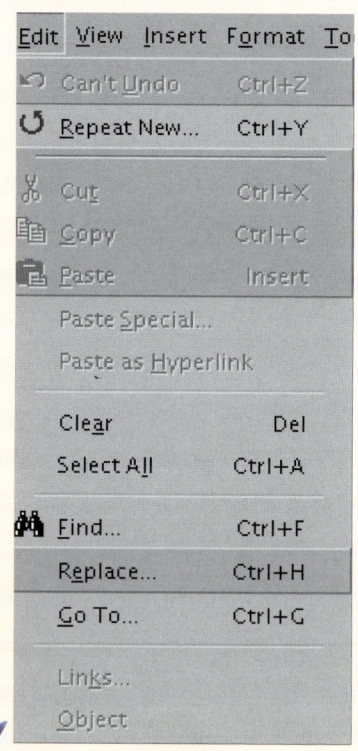

Look out for this logo. It means you only get this feature with Word 2000.

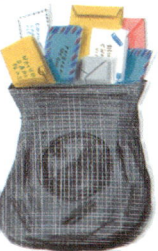

BACK TO BASICS

Let's get going by writing a letter or a note to someone. Most people love getting letters – so send a note to a friend or your gran or even Father Christmas to get you started.

LEARN TO ...

- type in your words
- use capitals
- start new lines
- correct mistakes
- move the cursor around
- print your work

Typing text

Start by putting your name and address at the top to show who the letter's from. With your blank Word document on-screen, type your name. All the letters are on the keyboard somewhere, as long as your name just has the normal letters in it. Of course, if your name is Héloïse or Åaronoviç you will need to go to 'Insert' on the menu bar and click on 'Symbol'. Look for the é or ç, or whatever you need, click on it, then press 'Insert'.

To get capitals LIKE THIS you need to press one of the 'Shift' keys at either side of the keyboard:

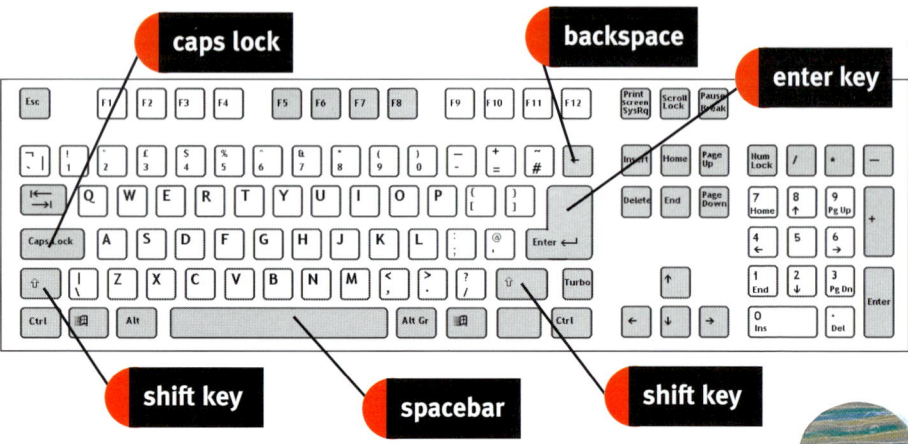

Watch this space

If you type more than one word – your first and your last name – you will need to leave a space between them. Press the 'Spacebar' only once to leave the right amount of space. At school, you might have been told to leave a finger space between words. On the computer, the 'Spacebar' adds just the right size finger space – you don't need to measure it on screen with your finger!

Wiggly lines

Your name might have a wiggly red line under it. That's because the computer thinks it's a spelling mistake. Computers aren't smart, and they don't have friends so they don't recognise many names. Don't worry about it – it doesn't matter and it won't print the wiggly line if you print out your document.

Always check the spelling when you see a wiggly red line, as sometimes it really will be a mistake.

This page has a spelligh mistake

Enter here

On the right-hand side of the keyboard is the 'Enter' key. When you press it, you will see that the cursor moves down to a new line.

Press 'Enter' every time you want to start a new line and you haven't got to the end of the line you're on. Try typing your address, pressing 'Enter' at the end of each line. It should look like this:

The Haunted Castle
Witchburn Lane
Dreadesville
DV12 8TY

If the letters don't look exactly like this don't worry, your computer is just using a different font.

The Haunted Castle¶
Witchburn Lane¶
Dreadesville¶
DV12 8TY¶
¶

You might see marks like these ¶. They show where 'Enter' has been pressed. They won't be printed. If you don't like them open the 'Tools' menu, choose 'Options' and find the 'View' tab. Click on the tick next to 'Paragraph marks'. This will get rid of them.

You might have used a different kind of text program at school that lets you click on the place on the page where you want to add your words or pictures. You can't do this with Word.

How about a date?

After you've put in the address press 'Enter' a couple of times to get some blank space and type the date. If you type it like this: 14 February 2002 and then press 'Enter', you might find Word messes it up:

14 February 2002-02-14

That's because it's seen the year and guessed you wanted to type the date, but didn't notice you'd already done it, so it's added 02-14 for February (02) 14th. To get rid of this, click this button on the toolbar: ↰

This means 'Undo' and it will get rid of whatever you (or the computer!) did last. It's a good way of clearing up mistakes and you will probably use it quite a lot.

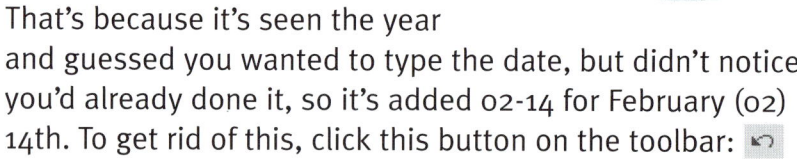

Dear Gran

Move the cursor down by pressing 'Enter' a few times and then type 'Dear Gran' (or whoever you're writing to). Press 'Enter' twice more and you can start typing your message. When you get to the end of the line, don't press 'Enter', but keep going. The text will jump to the beginning of the next line when you've run out of space. You should only press 'Enter' when you want to start a new paragraph or a new line in a list.

Signing off

When you've finished your message, put something at the end on a line on its own, like 'Best wishes', or 'Love from' (depending on who you're writing to!) and you've finished. You can sign your name in pen when you print the letter.

Whoops!

What if you make a mistake while you are typing? Look for the 'Backspace' key; it might have an arrow pointing left, or it might say 'Backspace'. Press this, and the last letter or number you typed will disappear and you can type the right one.

If you don't notice until you're a bit further down the page, move the mouse until the pointer is where the mistake is and click. The text cursor will jump there. You can move the cursor around using the arrow keys, too. Use the 'Backspace' key to get rid of the bit that's wrong and then type what you really wanted.

In the 'Tools' menu you'll find 'Spelling and Grammar'. If you click on it, Word will search through what you've written and let you know if you've made any spelling mistakes. Great, eh?

Printing it out

Unless you're going to invite your friend or your granny (or Father Christmas!) to come and read the letter on the screen, you need to get it out on a piece of paper so that you can send it. Give it a quick read through first and correct any mistakes, then find the print button on the toolbar. It looks like this: 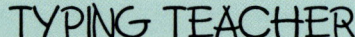 Click on it once to print your letter.

If your letter doesn't print out, make sure your printer is connected to the computer and turned on. Check it's got some paper in, too. If you see a message on screen that says something about printer drivers or connections, ask a grown-up to help you as it may mean some of the settings are wrong.

TYPING TEACHER

If you are a bit slow at typing, you can get a typing tutor program to help you speed up. This will teach you how to touch-type – type without looking at the keyboard – which looks pretty cool and means you can watch TV while you type! Check out the Whizz Kids website to find out where to get a typing tutor program.

STORY GO-ROUND

If you've got friends with Word, you can work together on a story. It can be really fun to do this. Someone starts the story off, saves their document, then passes it on to the next person. They add a bit, save it again, and pass it on to the next person.

LEARN TO...

- start a new document for your story
- save your work on the hard disc of your computer
- copy your work onto a floppy disc
- close a document
- open a story someone has given back to you

Sort out the rules

Agree who's going to start the story, the order in which you're all going to add to it, how many goes you each get and how much each person can write. If you work this out at the start, you're less likely to argue later on!

Getting started

Start a new document by clicking on this button: 🗋

Type a title for your story and press 'Enter' to start a new line.

Now start typing your story. Remember, press 'Enter' when you want to start a new paragraph, or to add a blank line, but not just because you've got to the end of the line on the screen – the computer will handle that for you.

Use 'Backspace' if you make any mistakes. When you've done your bit, you need to save the story and pass it on to the next person. Saving your work means that you will be able to get it back later, after you've closed it, stopped using Word or turned the computer off. It also means you can copy it onto another disc to give to someone else, or e-mail it to someone.

Pass it on

To save your work, click on the button that shows a picture of a floppy disc 💾. It's probably at the left of the tool bar, just beneath the 'File' and 'Edit' menus.

You'll see a 'Save As' box for you to tell the computer what to call your work and where to put it. Type a name for the story, or use the name the computer is offering. Call it something you will recognize easily, like 'Ghost story 1'.

Give your work a sensible name so that it's easy to find it again later. Think about it – if you put all your crayons in a box marked 'fred' you might not look in the right box next time you wanted them. Of course, if you want to keep your stuff secret, it might be a good idea to give it a misleading name. People are more likely to look at something called 'Top Secret Stuff' or 'My Best Story' than at something called 'Weather Reports' or 'Homework'.

Folders

It's a good idea to make a folder to keep your work sorted so that you can find it again, just as you might put your writing and pictures in paper folders on your desk. If you don't put your work in folders, it's like throwing all your stuff – everything you've got, whatever it is – into a huge box rather than putting it away properly. It's easy to put it away like this – but very hard to find something again later.

> If you already know about folders, you've probably got somewhere to put this story already.

19

Making new folders

If you haven't got a folder to keep your story in, you can create one now. At the top of the 'Save As' box is a button showing a folder with an arrow pointing upwards, like this. Click on this to move 'up' through the system of folders to the hard disc. It will show a picture like this: (C:) . Now click on the button with this picture, to make a new folder.

Give it a name that suits what you're going to put in it. If you share the computer, you might want to give it your own name so that you can keep your stuff separate from anyone else's.

Saved!

When you've picked the folder and typed a name, click on 'Save' and that's it. Now you can close Word and you can still get your story back again.

HELP BOX

Click on the button like this ☒ at the end of the menu line, to close your story. If you haven't got any of your writing on screen, clicking this will close down Word itself and you'll need to start it up again if you want to do more writing.

If you're going to let someone else use the same computer to carry on the story, or if you're going to e-mail it to someone, you've done all you need to save it.

Pop it on a floppy

If you want to give your story to someone to use on a different computer, and you can't e-mail it, you'll need to copy it onto a floppy disc. Put a floppy disc in the disc drive, then:

- Open the folder you saved the story in.
- Open a window for My Computer.

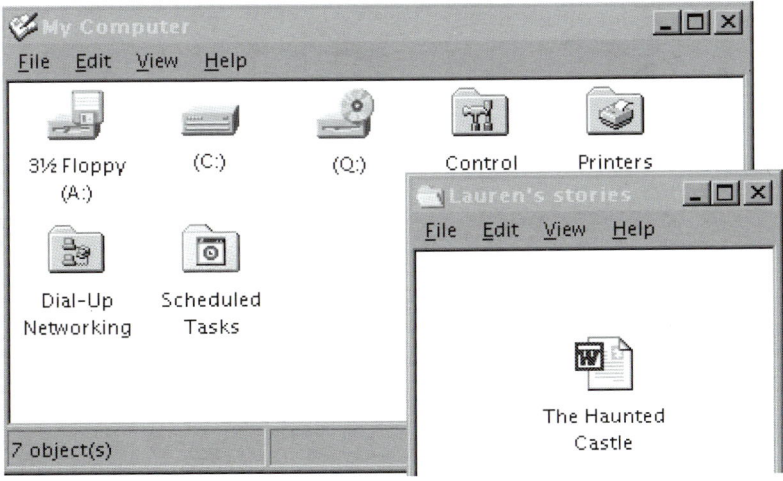

- Move the pointer over the icon for your story, hold down the left-hand mouse button and drag the icon onto the floppy disc icon. Let go of the mouse button and the story will be copied.

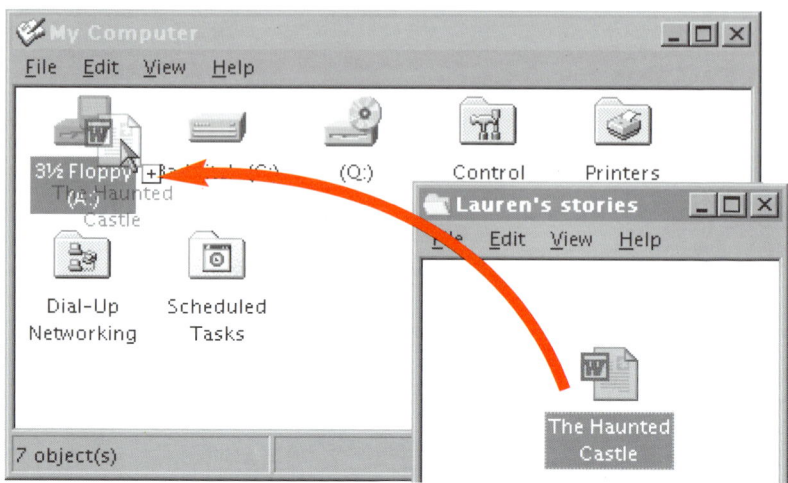

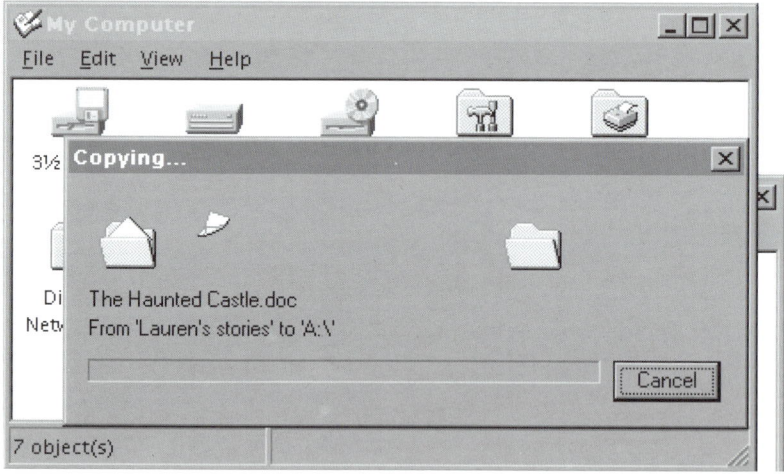

Your story is copied onto the floppy disc, but it will also stay on your hard disc. Take the floppy disc out of the drive and pass it on to the next person.

Your turn

When you get the story back on the disc, it's a good idea to copy it before you start work on your next bit – then you won't mess up the whole thing if you make a horrible mistake.

- Find a folder you want to put the story in.

- Open a window for the floppy disc (double-click on the floppy disc icon in the My Computer window).

- Move the pointer over the icon for the story, hold down the left-hand mouse button and drag it onto the icon for the folder. Now you can make your changes without worrying.

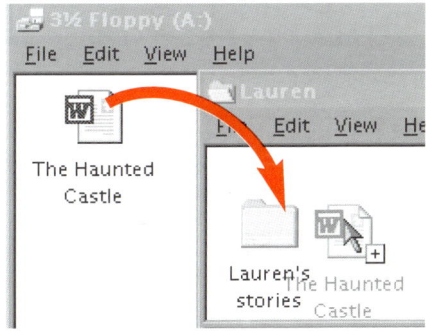

Keep a copy

It's a good idea to copy your best work onto another disc to keep a back-up copy. Then you can get it back if anything goes wrong with your hard disc. So it's useful to learn how to copy to a floppy disc.

Get into it

Open the story like this:

- Click on this button 📂, or choose 'Open' from the 'File' menu.

- Use this button ▼ and this button 📁 to move through the folders on your disc. To open a folder shown in the list you can see, double-click on it.

- When you find the story, double click on it, or click once and then on 'Open'.

Add your next bit to the story and save it by clicking on the 'Save' button again. This time, the computer knows what to call it and where to put it, so you don't need to do anything else. But, you can choose 'Save As' from the 'File' menu and change the name so that you can keep both versions.

Now copy it back onto the floppy disc to pass on to the next person. If you're using the same name, a message will appear asking if you want to replace the copy on the disc – click 'OK'. Time to pass it on again...

HELP BOX

If you're working on something long and difficult, it's a good idea to save it every 10 minutes or so – that way, you won't have to do too much again if there's a power cut or you make a mistake.

TOP SECRET

Have you ever wanted a secret code so that your mum, brother or sister can't read the notes you send to your friends? Here's an easy way to make what you write look like complete gobbledegook – but you and your mates can untangle your message easily!

LEARN TO...

- change your messages into code
- make a code crib sheet
- change code back into English

How to do it

You start by typing your note. It could be anything. Here's ours:

'meet me at the shed at 3pm'

- Now we'll change the font so that it looks like just pictures or symbols:

¡▪▪▭ ¡▪ ✓▭ ▭◫▪ ?◫▪♥ ✓▭ ◀🚗¡

Here's how to do it:

- Select the text of your message. Do this by putting the cursor at the start, holding down the mouse button and dragging over it so that it changes colour, then taking your finger off the mouse button.

meet me at the shed at 3 pm

- Open the 'Format' menu, and click on 'Font'. A box appears for you to choose how your text looks.

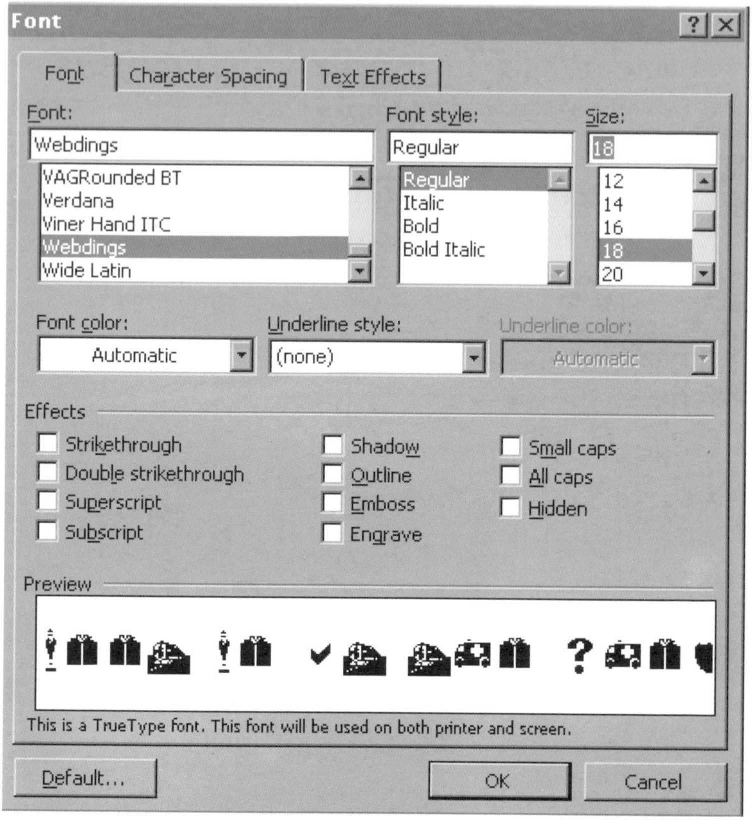

Font			? X

Font	Character Spacing	Text Effects

Font:
Webdings

| VAGRounded BT |
| Verdana |
| Viner Hand ITC |
| Webdings |
| Wide Latin |

Font style:
Regular

| Regular |
| Italic |
| Bold |
| Bold Italic |

Size:
18

| 12 |
| 14 |
| 16 |
| 18 |
| 20 |

Font color:
Automatic

Underline style:
(none)

Underline color:
Automatic

Effects

- [ ] Strikethrough
- [ ] Double strikethrough
- [ ] Superscript
- [ ] Subscript
- [ ] Shadow
- [ ] Outline
- [ ] Emboss
- [ ] Engrave
- [ ] Small caps
- [ ] All caps
- [ ] Hidden

Preview

This is a TrueType font. This font will be used on both printer and screen.

Default...		OK	Cancel

- There's a list of fonts at the top. Pick one like Webdings, Wingdings or Dingbats to see what it looks like. When you've found one you like, click on 'OK' and your message turns into code. Magic!

If it's hard to see, you can make the original text a bit bigger.

- When you've finished, click on this button to print a copy of your message: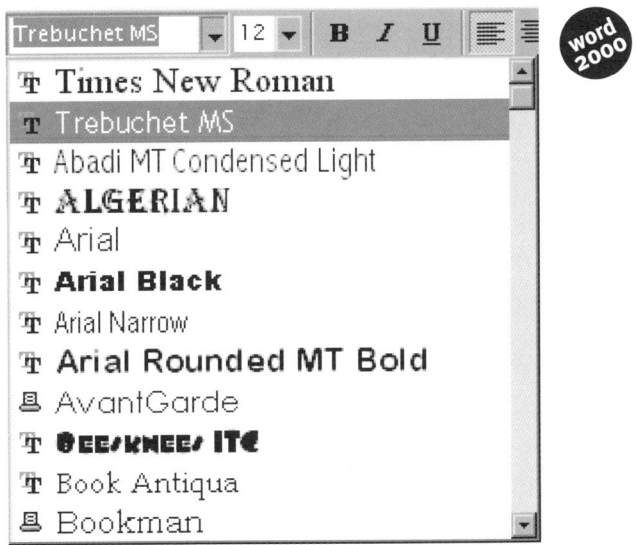

Drop-down gorgeous

If you're using Word 2000, you can also see what the fonts look like in the drop-down list from the tool bar, so you could use this instead.

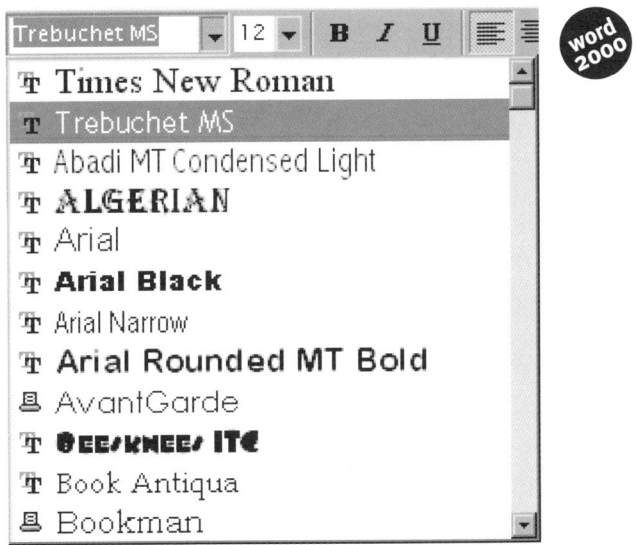

Untangling by hand

How's your friend going to understand the message? You need a quick reference card. Here's how to make one:

- Start a new document and type out the whole alphabet in it, with each letter on a different line. Do this by typing a letter, then press 'Enter', typing the next letter and so on.

- Now type the numbers 0–9 in the same way, and then any punctuation you plan to use.

- When you've done it, select it all (drag over it, or you can use 'Select All' from the 'Edit' menu) and change it to the font you've used for your code.

- Finally, you need to print this out and write next to each code letter what the real letter or number is.

Now you have a key to the code you use to decode all your messages!

It's easiest if you agree to use only small or capital letters and numbers. If you are going to use both capitals and small letters for your coded letters, you'll need to do both on your crib sheet too. You'd better leave spaces between the letters instead of starting new lines, or it will go onto more than one page.

Untangling by computer

The easiest way to decode your messages is to pass them around on disc, or e-mail them as attachments. Then you can read them just by selecting all the text and changing it back to an ordinary font like Arial or Times New Roman.

If you have more than one document open on screen, you can switch between them by clicking on the name of the one you want in the Windows menu.

If you want to know about e-mailing Word documents, check out our 'Whizz Kids: e-mail wizard' book.

29

LET'S PARTY!

Having a party? Save money on expensive invitations by printing your own. You can make little labels for the party bags, too!

LEARN TO...

- add a picture to your invitation
- change the size and colour of the words
- move the words to the middle of the line
- add a 'tear here' line to your invitation

What's what

Start by thinking about your invitations. Do you want a picture? What colours do you want to use? Do you have a colour printer, or will you need to colour them in yourself afterwards? Don't forget a tear-off slip for your friends to say whether they're coming or not!

Find-a-pic

First, you need to find or draw a picture to use on your invitation. If you've got a painting program, you can use this to create a picture. Alternatively, you could use some clip art. These are pictures that come with Word. You can also use something you've scanned in, or a picture you've taken with your digital camera.

When you're ready to begin, start a new document, and put your picture in. Here's how:

- Open the 'Insert' menu, move the pointer across 'Picture', and choose either 'Clip Art' or 'From File', depending on whether you want to use a picture of your own or clip art.

- If you choose 'Picture', you'll have to work your way through the folders to find the picture you want.

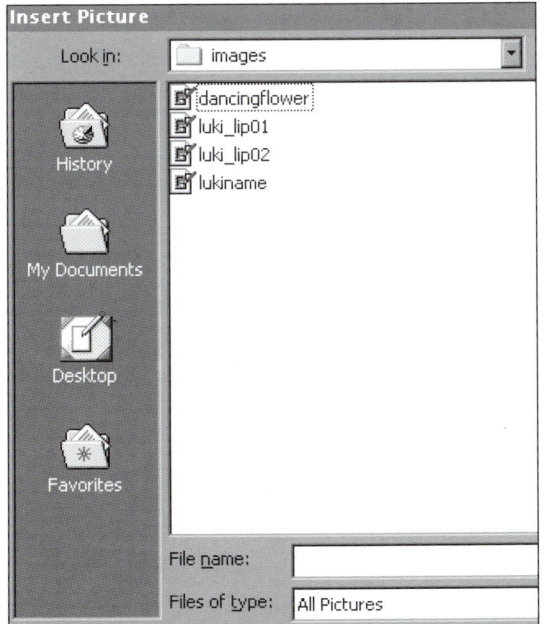

- If you choose 'Clip Art', you will first have to choose the type of picture you want, and then look through them for the particular one you want.

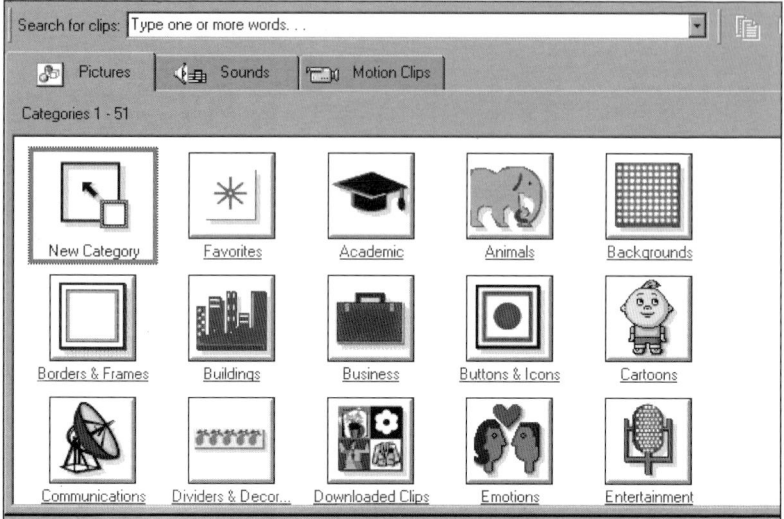

- When you find one you like, click on it and then click the top option in the menu that opens. This copies it into your invitation.

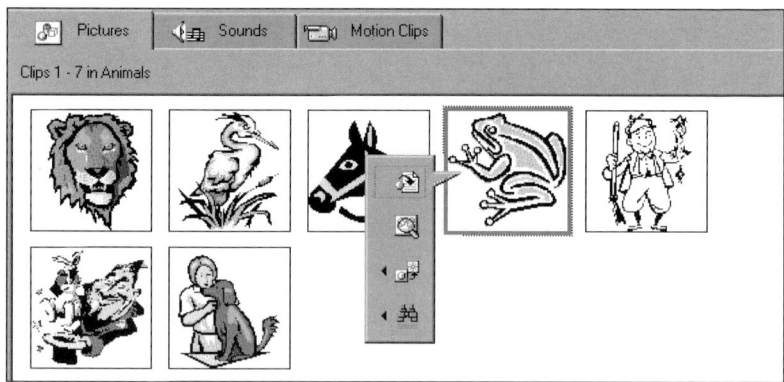

- The picture will appear on the page. Leave it where it is for now and press 'Enter' to get to the next line.

Whizzy words

Work out what you want to say and type it in. It will look boring to start with, but don't worry, you can soon jazz it up.

Lauren's 9th Birthday Party!
Please come to my slimy pondlife party
on
1st October
at
The Haunted Castle
Dress: slimy, or pond-related

RSVP
Phone me: 07882 144328
Email me: lauren@woppa2000.co.uk
I can / cannot come to your party
From:

You found out in the chapter 'Top Secret' how to select words and change the font. Now you're going to select words and change the font, colour and size.

First, select the words you want to change.

You can change the size and the font from the menus that drop down from the toolbar. But as you're likely to change these and the colour all together, open the 'Format' menu and choose 'Font'. Here you can choose a font, a colour and a size all at once.

HELP BOX

Remember, you can select a single word by double-clicking on it, and a line by clicking in the left margin next to it. You can also select a whole paragraph by triple-clicking on it.

More buttons

You can also use these buttons on the toolbar to change the text to bold or italic or add underlining: **B** *I* U

Looks better, doesn't it?

Into the middle

Now you need to move the lines to the middle of the page. You do this using the 'Center' button. It's like this: ☰

You can select all the lines, or click in a line and then on the 'Center' button to move one line at a time. You can also centre the picture you added at the start.

If the 'Center' button isn't on the toolbar, open the 'Format' menu and choose 'Paragraph', then pick 'Centered' from the drop-down 'Alignment' menu.

Alignment:	Left ▾
Left
Indentation	Centered
Left:	Right
Justified

Turn to the right

Try out 'Right', too. This moves all the lines so that they end at the same point on the right-hand side of the page. 'Left' puts it all back where it was.

You can pick a good page border for the whole invitation, (find out how to do this in the next chapter 'Nice notes') and this is what your finished invitation could look like.

RSVP

Next you need to put in a bit for a reply, in a tear-off slip at the bottom. This needs a dotted edge to show where to cut it. You could do this with a row of dots or dashes, but there's a quicker way.

- Make sure you've got a few blank line spaces between the invitation and information in the tear-off slip. Click at the start of the slip just above where you've written RSVP.

- Click to the left of one of the blank lines in the middle of the space. You will see a little black block which shows you've selected a line with no words in it.

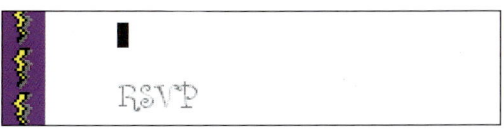

- Open the 'Format' menu and choose 'Borders and Shading'. Make sure it's showing the 'Borders' tab, and pick a dotted border style from the panel in the middle.

Below, you can see what this looks like. As there are lines all around, this will add a box around your blank line. You don't want this, so click on the buttons or the picture of the borders, to turn off the bottom, left and right borders. Now it shows just the top border, which is fine, so click 'OK'.

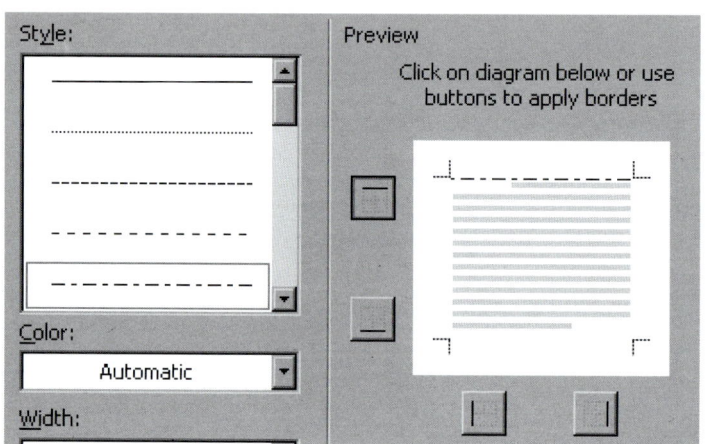

Print it out

You're going to invite more than one person to the party, so you'll need more than one invitation. If you click the print button, you just get one. To get more, open the 'File' menu and choose 'Print'. Find the section that says 'Copies' and put the number you want into the box.

NICE NOTES

Writing letters is more fun if you've got nice notepaper – and if you've got a computer, you can always have nice notepaper – you can make your own.

LEARN TO...

- add a plain border
- add an arty border
- make a template you can use over and over again

Personal touch

Grown-ups often use paper that has their name and address already printed on it – it saves writing these out every time. You can do this too, but you don't need to stop there. You can have nice pictures or borders on your paper. You can print these in colour or, for a more personal touch, print an outline picture and colour it in when you've finished. Then it can be different colours every time.

Home time

Start with your name and address. Type them at the top of the page, pressing 'Enter' to get each line of your address to start on a new line. When you've done it, use what you've learned already to select the text and change the font, the size and the colour.

Take me to the border

Now add a border around your page. If you're using Word in Office 2000, there's an easy way to do this.

- Open the 'Format' menu and choose 'Borders and Shading'.

- When the box appears, click on the tab 'Page Borders'. Below you can see some ordinary borders, though they can be quite nice if you give them a bright colour.

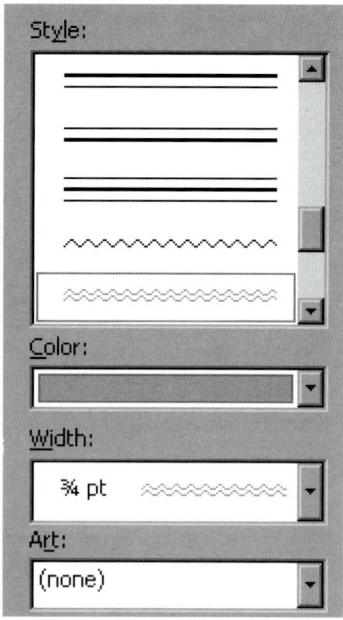

Let's get arty

Best of all are the 'art' borders. Here's how to find them:

- Find the line that says 'Art': and click on the button to the right of the space.

- There's a drop-down menu of patterns that you can scroll through until you find something you like. Click on the one you want to use.

- The border you choose is shown on the little picture of a page to the right. On this, you can click on any of the edges to turn the border on or off – so you could have it just at the top and bottom, or just at the sides, or all the way round.

Try out a few of the borders until you've found one you like. Before you type a letter using your notepaper, save it so that you can use it again and again. Make sure you choose a file name you will recognize later.

Smarty pants

Instead of just saving your notepaper, you can save it in a special way so that you don't accidentally save over it when you type a letter.

- Choose 'Save As' from the 'File' menu, and click on the arrow next to the space 'Save as Type'.

- In the menu, choose 'Document Template' and then save your file.

If you're using Word 2000, don't change the place Word wants to save it to. It needs to put your templates here so that it can find them again when you need them.

Make no mistake

When you want to write a letter, choose 'New' from the 'File' menu and you'll see a list of the document templates

you have. Double-click on your notepaper to start a new letter – and you won't be able to save your letter with the same name and lose your notepaper by mistake.

DRAMA QUEENS (AND KINGS)

Ever had to learn lines for a play and found it hard to follow your part? Next time you put on a play with your friends, or have to learn your lines for the school play, use **Word** to make it simple.

LEARN TO...

- set text styles
- make indents
- do keyboard shortcuts
- work the tab key

What style!

You can make your part stand out by making it a different colour (if you have a colour printer), or making it bold, or bigger. The quickest way to do this is using 'styles'.

A style is a group of settings that you can make all at once – it's a good way of making bits of your work look the same without having to remember what you did.

You can set a named style for each character – you can use the characters' names as the style names to make it easier to remember. You can make each character's words look distinctive. Perhaps the wicked witch has green italic words, and the beautiful princess has bold, blue words. It's then easy to see where your part comes in.

Setting your style

This is how to set the style you want:

- In the 'Format' menu, click on 'Style'. The box shows the styles you've got already.

- Click on the 'New' button to create a style for the first character. Use the character's name for the style name, so you can identify it easily.

- Click on the 'Format' button and choose 'Font' from the menu that appears.

- Choose how you want the first character's words to appear – maybe red, or bold, or big, or underlined, or even all of these. The things you pick are used for the sample words in the box, so you can see how it will look. Click on 'OK' when you're happy with what you've chosen, but don't close the style dialogue box yet.

Doing indents

Now set an indent so that the character's name is in the margin and their words are a bit further across to make it clearer – it's how real play scripts look. To do this, click the 'Format' button again and choose 'Paragraph'. In the box under 'Special', choose 'Hanging' and set the number in the next box to 3 cm.

This should give you enough room for the names, but if they are very long you can set a larger number. Click 'OK' when you've done it.

HELP BOX

A hanging indent means that the first line of the paragraph starts at the left-hand side, but the second and later lines start a bit further across the page.

Here is what your text should look like when you have set the style and put in your indents:

CASPER   **Oh no! he's getting away! Quick, in the boat!**

VERA   No, there's a hole in the boat – it'll sink and we'll be eaten by sharks.

          Sharks start to circle

Doing shortcuts

To speed up using your style, set a keyboard shortcut. This will be a control key, such as 'Ctrl' or 'Alt', with a letter or number key. So 'Alt-3' would mean pressing the 'Alt' key and the '3' key at the same time. Here's how to do it:

- From the 'New Style' box, click 'Shortcut Key' and then press a control key and a letter or number key together.

- Click 'Close', then 'Apply'.

When you want to use your style, either for new text or to change text that's already there, just press both keys at the same time and the text will change. Set up a style for each character, or change just your own lines in the play so that they're easier to follow.

Changing styles

If you've typed the play already, click in each paragraph and change it to the right style, either picking it from the 'Style' menu on the toolbar or using the key shortcut you've set up. If you haven't typed the text yet, pick the style for each character's words before you type them.

Keeping tabs

After you've typed the character's name at the start of the line, press the 'Tab' key on the keyboard and the cursor will jump to the position of the indent – all the character's lines will line up. If a character has more than one paragraph at a time, just press 'Tab' at the start of each paragraph to keep the lines in the right place.

HELP BOX

If you've already got your play typed in, put the cursor after the character's name each time and press 'Tab' to move their words across to the right place on the page. If there's an extra space before the words start, delete it.

Then you're all ready to be a star of stage and screen!

ALL I WANT IS...

Having trouble sorting your Christmas or birthday list? Let the computer help you make it look clearer and more exciting!

LEARN TO...

- make a list with numbers
- move the lines around to change the order
- make a list with splodges or pictures or even movies!

Wish list

Start with the title. It might be 'What I want for my Birthday' or 'Christmas list', and press 'Enter'.

You've seen in the last chapter 'Drama Queens' how to create a style that you can reuse. But Word also comes with some styles set up for you to use already. There is a set of styles for headings, so that you can add titles and subheadings to your work easily, but they can be pretty boring.

Jazz it up

Here is how to make the letters more interesting. Click on the title you've just typed, and then on the arrow button next to 'Normal' on the toolbar, to show the list of styles. Choose 'Heading 1'. Now open the 'Format' menu and choose 'Style'. You can make the heading much more interesting.

Make sure 'Heading 1' is the style highlighted in the list, then click the 'Format' button. In the menu, choose 'Font', and then click on the 'Text Effects' tab. If you have Word 2000 check out 'Sparkle Text' . Go back to the 'Font' tab and set the size, colour and font for a really good effect.

48 Fur lined wellies, 49...

You can get the computer to add numbers to your wish-list. Type your list, with each thing on a different line, then select the text and click on this button to add the numbers:

Shake it up

If you just typed the things you want in the order you thought of them, you might have the most important at the bottom. Better re-order your list so that you don't just get the three things at the top! Here's how:

- Move the pointer to the left-hand edge of the list until it turns into an arrow, then click once. The whole line will be selected. If the thing you're choosing goes over more than one line, press the left-hand mouse button and drag the pointer down to select all the lines you want to move.

- Now move the pointer over the selected text and it will change to a red arrow. Press the mouse button and hold it down. The pointer now has a shadowy cursor at the point of the arrow and a shadowy square at the other end. This shows that you are moving a block of text. It will be put in at the position of the pointer when you take your finger off the mouse button.

If you find this hard to do, you can click the 'Cut' button  , then put the cursor where you want to add the line and click the 'Paste' button .

You can select a single word by double-clicking on it, or a whole block of text by holding down the left-hand mouse button and dragging over the part you want to select. If you select the wrong bit, just click somewhere else and it will be deselected.

Not just numbers

If you want lots of stuff for Christmas, you might not want to use a list with numbers. If it's too obvious you want 43 things, your list won't go down too well. Use bullets instead – a special character at the start of each line of your list. Then at least your mum has to count the lines to find out how much you want!

Type your list, select the text and click on this button:

> You'll get a round black blob next to each line in your list.

Cool blobs

Round black blobs aren't very exciting so instead of bullets you could choose a different character, or even a picture or a movie – how about a Christmas tree with flashing lights at the start of each line? (Looks cool on screen, but remember that if you print it out, the lights won't flash.) Here's how: Open the 'Format' menu and choose 'Bullets and Numbering'. You can:

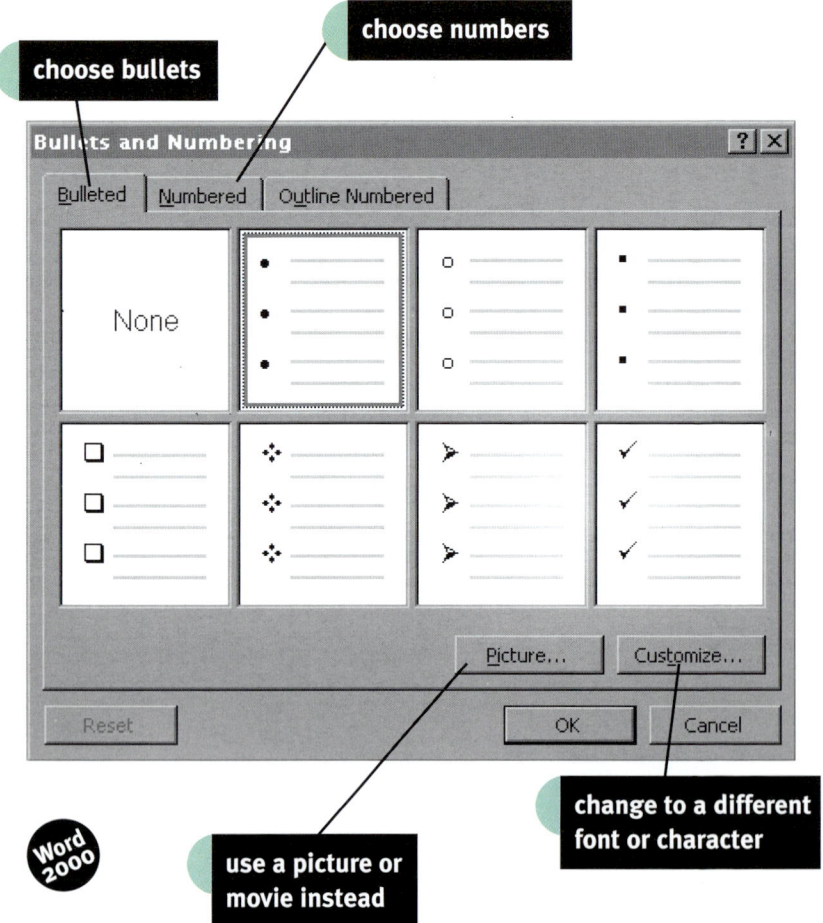

choose numbers

choose bullets

use a picture or movie instead

change to a different font or character

click here to choose moving bullets

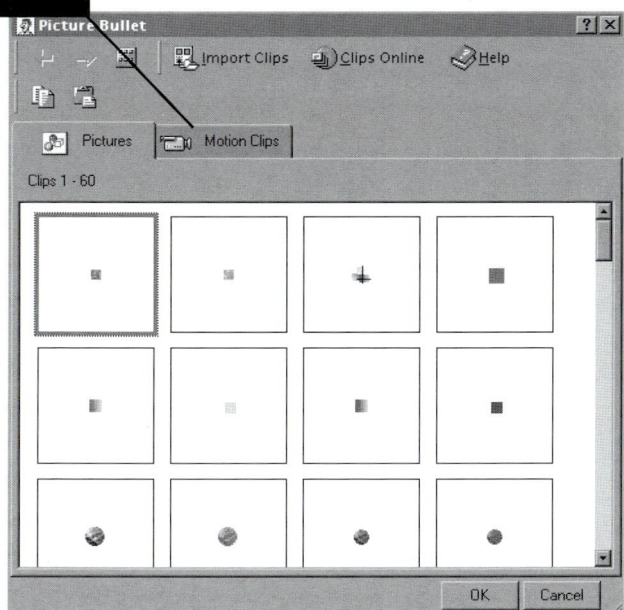

These are picture bullets.

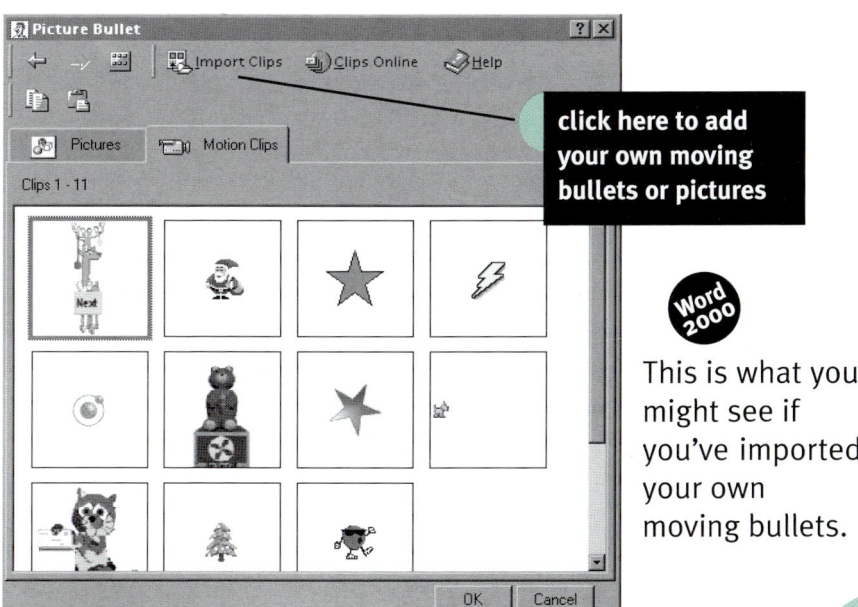

click here to add your own moving bullets or pictures

This is what you might see if you've imported your own moving bullets.

Hyper hints

If your mum or dad (or Santa Claus) is going to read your list on the computer, you can even add links to websites that describe what you want, or where the goodies can be ordered on-line. If you type the web address, Word will convert it to a hyperlink for you and will start your web browser and go on-line when Santa clicks on it!

What I want for Christmas.

Furby (www.toyland.co.uk/furby_bits.htm)
Pokemon Yellow
Personal organizer

THANK YOU VERY MUCH FOR...

Do you get sick of writing thank you letters and end up writing letters that are really boring or too short? If you do them on the computer, you can write a long, interesting letter, because you only need to write it once!

LEARN TO...

- change the words you've written
- add new bits to an old letter

Set up the page

If you've made some nice notepaper, you can use that. (See the chapter called 'Nice Notes'.) To start a new letter using your notepaper template, open the 'File' menu and choose 'New'. Click on the name of your notepaper and on 'OK' and you can start.

If you didn't make a template, just open the notepaper document. It's a good idea to save it with a different name immediately so that you don't lose the blank copy. Open the 'File' menu and choose 'Save As', then change the name shown before you click 'Save'.

Get writing...

Now, type your first thank you letter. You are only going to type most of it once, so you can make it quite long and interesting. Make sure you put all the bits about the person you're writing to, or the present they gave you, in one or two places so that you can find it easily to change it.

Dear granny

Thank you for the Gameboy game you sent for my birthday. It's just what I wanted – now I have all the latest games and I'm top of the Gameboy league at school.

On my birthday we went to Legoland, and Jacqui and James came too. The weather was horrid but we had a great time.

Now save this letter and print it out.

Next!

To do the next one, you just need to change the name and the present.

Select the name of the person you've just written to and, while it is selected, just type the next name you want. The old one will be gone, and the new name will be in its place.

Do the same with the bit about the present – select it and type over it.

54

If this doesn't work, open the 'Tools' menu and choose 'Options'. Click on the 'Edit' tab and click on 'Typing replaces selection' to put a tick in the box, then click on 'OK'.

Be careful

Check what you've written to make sure it still makes sense and there isn't anything else in the letter that makes it look silly or makes it clear that you've just changed an old letter. If you've kept all the bits about the person and the present together, it's easy to check this and change it if you need to. Can you see what's wrong with the letter below?

Dear uncle Adrian

Thank you for the Newt Keeping Handbook you sent for my birthday. It's just what I wanted - now I have all the latest games and I'm top of the Gameboy league at school.

On my birthday we went to Legoland, and Jacqui and James came too. The weather was horrid but we had a great time.

Print your letter, and move on to the next... it will be done in no time!

Delete and insert

Whatever you're working on, if there's a bit you need to take out completely, select it and then press the 'Delete' key. If you want to put an extra bit in, click where you want it to start and begin typing. If it types over the text in front of the cursor, you can change this. Open the 'Tools' menu and choose 'Options'. Click on the 'Edit' tab and click on the tick next to 'Overtype mode' so it disappears, to stop it doing this.

WANTED – GOOD POSTERS!

There are lots of things you might need posters for – to advertise your club or band, or get help looking for a lost pet, for example. You can make great posters on the computer, and you can print lots of copies really quickly.

LEARN TO...

- make a bigger page (if your printer can print on bigger paper)
- add special text
- use symbols as pictures

Poster paper

Some printers will take A3 paper. This is twice the size of the A4 paper you usually use. If your printer can do this – and you have some A3 paper – you can make big posters. If not, don't worry – you can make an A4 poster and if you want to, you can take it to a photocopy shop to get it enlarged.

If you are going to make an A3 poster, you need to tell the computer you're doing this before you start. Here's how:

- Start a new document.
- Open the 'File' menu and choose 'Page Setup'.
- Click on the 'Paper Size' tab and choose 'A3' from the drop-down menu.

It won't be in the menu if your printer can't cope with it.

HELP BOX

You can also use the 'Page setup' dialogue box to set the margins – how much space will be left around your words and pictures. Click the 'Margins' tab to do this.

Wicked and wild words

You've already found out how to make your text big and bold, change the colour and the font, and put it in the middle of the page or on the right. You know how to put pictures on the page, too. Another option in 'Picture' from the 'Insert' menu is 'Word Art', which is a picture made of words – it's a really cool text effect.

Making Word Art work

Here's how to add a whizzy title to your poster. Choose 'Word Art' and you'll get a box showing different types of text effect. Click on the style you want and on 'OK'. Next, type your words. You can choose a font and a size to use.

Once you've added the Word Art, a new tool bar appears for you to make changes to it:

You can twist it around, change the colours, change the wording, make it vertical, set how the other text runs around it, or pick a different style.

You can move the Word Art around the poster by dragging it.

Text or Art?

Word Art is one way of making words look like pictures. You can also use the symbols and pictures in some of the fonts you might have looked at in the 'Top Secret' chapter. This is an easy way to add pictures like smileys.

Finding font pictures

To find the pictures you want from a font, open the 'Insert' menu and choose 'Symbol'. It opens a box that shows you all the characters in a font. Use the drop-down menu at the top to switch to a different font. The pictures are a bit small, but each is shown bigger if you click on it. When you've found something you like, click 'Insert' and it will be added to your poster where your cursor is. Click 'Close' when you've finished.

HELP BOX

You can change the size of the symbol you've added by selecting it and using the drop-down menu on the toolbar for text size. Don't forget you can change the colour, too.

Here are some pictures you can get from fonts:

You might be able to get some really cool pictures if you've got funky fonts on your computer.

Don't forget you can use ordinary text and pictures on your poster, too – or maybe that's too dull!

GLOSSARY

bold
Text in heavy type, like **this.**

bullet
A blob, shape or picture at the start of each line of items in a list.

caret
The flashing line that shows where your typing will appear in a document or a form on the screen.

CD-ROM
Compact disc which contains information you can use on your computer.

clip art
Ready made pictures available from the World Wide Web or on CD-ROM.

cursor
Flashing block or line that shows where your typing will appear in a document or a form on the screen.

dialogue box
Box that appears on the screen with spaces for you to give answers to questions the computer is asking you, or buttons to choose what you want the computer to do.

document
A computer file with your text and pictures in it.

double-click
Press and let go of a mouse button twice rapidly.

drag
Hold down a mouse button and move the mouse so that you 'drag' over an area of the screen. You might use this to select or move something on the screen.

drive
Any kind of computer storage device that you can save your work on or read files from. A drive works with a disc - so a hard disc drive operates a hard disc, a floppy disc drive works with a floppy disc and a CD-ROM drive works with CD-ROMs.

e-mail
Electronic mail. This allows you to send messages, and often also pictures and other information, to anyone else who has an e-mail address. The information is sent over the Internet.

folder
A special space to store work or programs on the computer. Organising your work into folders helps you to keep track of it.

font
A design for letters and numbers, sometimes called a typeface. Some different fonts are: Times, Courier, Arial, *Comic Sans*.

hard disc
Large disc fitted inside your computer that stores your work and programs.

hyperlink
A link to another document, often a World Wide Web page. The linked words are usually shown in colour and often underlined. Clicking on the link opens the linked document.

icon
Little picture used to represent something, like a document, a disc, or an option (such as saving or printing your work).

import
Copy a file into somewhere. You might import a picture into a document, which will add a copy of it on the page, or you might import movie clips into your set of bullets so that you can choose them in your document.

indent
Start text some way in from the left-hand margin of the page.

italic
Text that slants, like *these words do.*

menu
A list of options from which you can make a choice.

paste
Put words into your document that you have copied or removed from somewhere else.

scroll
Move through a document or list that is too long or wide to show on the screen all at once.

select
Choose a word, group of words, document or something else, so that you can carry out some activity with it. You usually select something by clicking on it or dragging over it.

shortcut
Quick route to open a document, folder, program or activity. A shortcut may be an icon you click on, or a couple of keys you press together on the keyboard.

style
Group of settings for text that are always used together. Using styles makes it quicker and easier to get your work looking consistent.

tab
Pressing the Tab key moves the cursor to a set place on the line you are typing.

template
Outline of a document that you can use to make lots of documents that look the same. You can set up the styles you use for text, add a picture, add some words that you want in all the documents, and make settings for the page.

toolbar
Strip of buttons somewhere on the screen.

INDEX

addresses on letters 13, 38
'Alt' key 44

'Backspace' key 12, 15, 18
birthday lists 46–52
bold text 34, 62
borders 35, 36, 38–39
bullets 49, 50–51, 62

capital letters 12
caret 9, 62
CD-ROM 62
'Center' button 34
changing text 54–55
Christmas lists 46–52
clip art 31–32, 62
closing documents 20
codes 25–29
colour changes 33
control keys 44
copying to and from floppy discs 21–22, 23
'Ctrl' key 44
cursor 9, 62
'Cut' button 48

dates on letters 14
decoding messages 28–29
deleting text 56
dotted edges 35–36
'double-click' procedure 62
'drag' procedure 62

e-mails 21, 62
'Enter' key 12, 13, 18

floppy discs 21–23
folders 19–20, 62
font pictures 60–61
fonts 26–27, 33, 42, 47, 62

hyperlinks 52, 62

icons 62–63
'import' procedures 63
indents 43, 45, 63
inserting text 56
italic text 34, 63

keyboard shortcuts 44

'Left' alignment 34
letter writing 11–16, 53–56

margins 58, 63
menus 6–7, 8, 9, 10, 63
mistakes, checking for 12–13, 15–16, 55
moving text 48–49

naming documents 18–19
naming folders 20
'new document' button 18
notepaper 37–40, 53
numbering lists 47

'Office' toolbar 6
opening documents 24
ordering lists 48–49
overtyping 56

'Page Setup' box 58
paper sizes 57–58
paragraph marks 13
party invitations 30–36
'Paste' button 48, 63
picture bullets 50, 51
pictures 5, 31–32, 58–61
play scripts 41–45
posters 57–61
printing documents 5, 16, 36
'Programs' menu 6–7

quick buttons 8, 9

re-ordering lists 48–49
'Right' alignment 34
RSVP slips 35

saving work 18–20, 24, 40, 53
scrolling 63
selecting words 25, 27, 28, 48–49, 63
'Shift' keys 12, 27
shortcuts 6, 44, 63
signing off letters 15
size of words 33
spacebar 12
special letters 11
spelling mistakes 12–13, 16
'Start' menu 6–7
starting new documents 18
starting up computers 6
starting up Word 6–7
story writing 17–24
styles 41–45, 46–47, 63
symbols 11, 60–61

'Tab' key 45, 63
tear-off slips 35–36
templates 40, 63
'Text Effects' tab 47
thank you letters 53–56
toolbars 6, 16, 63
typing 11–12
'Typing replaces selection' option 55

underlined text 34
'Undo' button 14

website links 52
Word Art 58–59
Word 2000 10, 27, 38, 51